AUTOMOTIVE

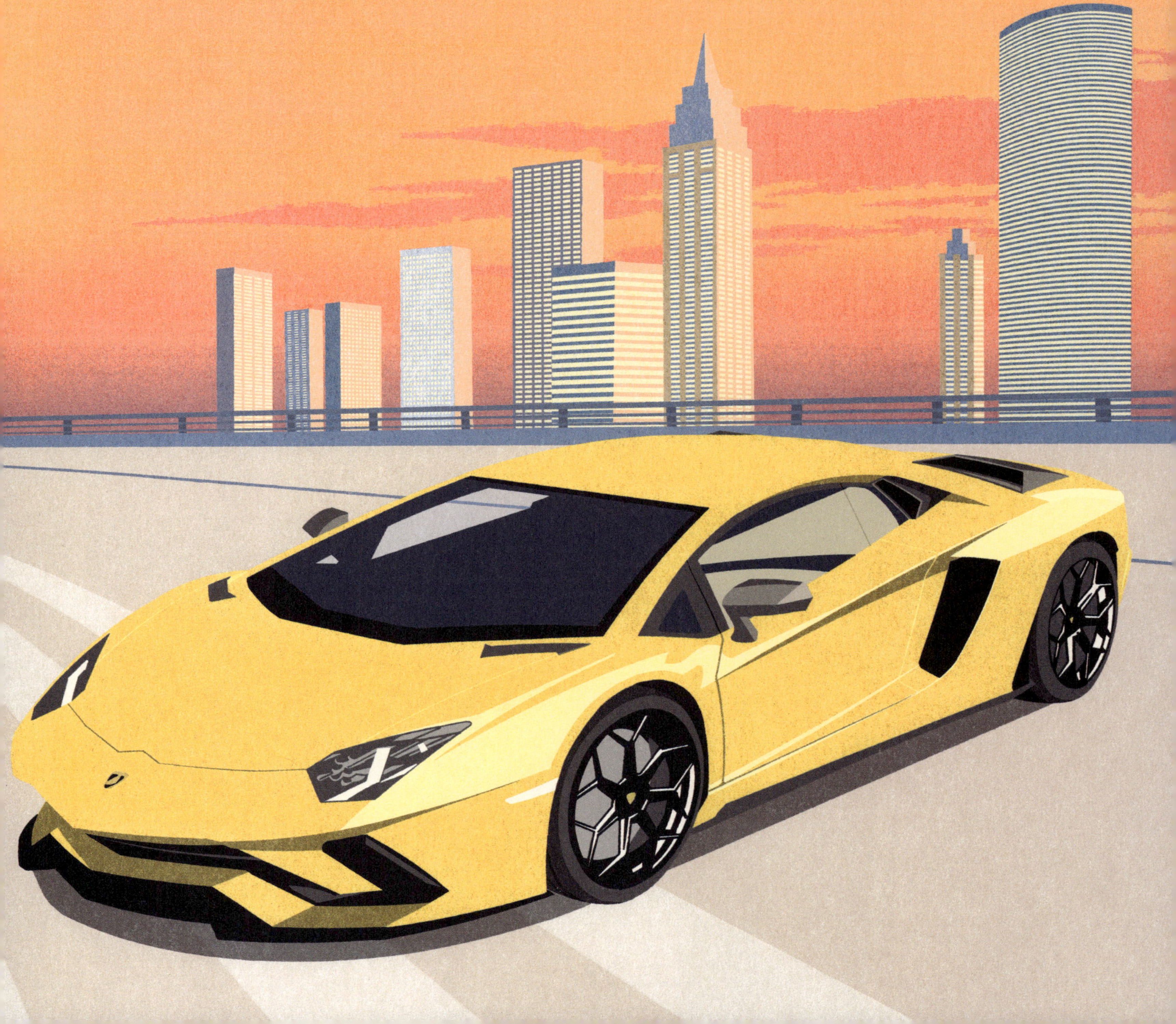

For Aleena, Asmaa, Lins, Liz, Lucy and Sarah – the Farshore team! M.R.

BIG PICTURE PRESS

First published in the UK in 2023 by Big Picture Press,
an imprint of Bonnier Books UK,
4th Floor, Victoria House,
Bloomsbury Square, London, WC1B 4DA
Owned by Bonnier Books
Sveavägen 56, Stockholm, Sweden
www.bonnierbooks.co.uk

All illustrations based on photographs. The publisher would like to thank the following:

FRONT COVER: 1973 FerrariDino 246 GTS. Photograph supplied by Motoring Picture Library, used by permission. INTERIORS: p8 The Monte Carlo Rally, Monaco, 1954. Photograph by NATIONAL MOTOR MUSEUM / HERITAGE IMAGES/SCIENCE PHOTO LIBRARY, used by permission. p14 Rally Finland, Photograph by Nacho Mateo/Shutterstock, used by permission. p18 Lambourghini, 2017. Photograph by Kaukola Photography/Shutterstock, used by permission. p20 Silver Ghost. Photograph by Tim Scott/Fluid Images, used by permission. p24 Isle of Man TT race, UK 2016. Photograph by JazzyGeoff/Shutterstock, used by permission. p26 Daytona 500. Photograph by Kevin Norris/Shutterstock, used by permission. p28 Citroën Karin. Photograph http://www.citroenet.org.uk/prototypes/karin/karin.html, courtesy of Arthur Fryling. p30, Proteus Bluebird CN7. Photograph supplied by Motoring Picture Library, used by permission. p30 ThrustSSC. Photograph by Andrew Paterson/Alamy Stock Photo, used by permission. p30 Thrust2. Photograph by Marc Tielemans/Alamy Stock Photo, used by permission. p34 Monaco Grand Prix, 2019. Photograph by cristiano barni, used by permission. p38 Peterbilt 289. Photograph by Carmen K. Sisson/Cloudybright/Alamy Stock Photo, used by permission. p40 BIGFOOT®, Monster Truck. BIGFOOT® is a registered trademark of BIGFOOT 4X4, Inc., 2286 Rose Ln., Pacific, MO 63069 USA Bigfoot4x4.com. © 2022 All Rights Reserved. Photographer: Danny Maass. Photo used with permission. p46 Le Mans, France, 2019. Photograph by Max Earey/Shutterstock, used by permission. p50 Ford Deuce Hot Rod, USA, 2012. Photograph by Bruce Alan Bennett/Shutterstock, used by permission. p54 The Beast (Cadillac One). Photograph supplied by GM Heritage Archive, used by permission.

1 3 5 7 9 10 8 6 4 2

ISBN 978-1-80078-317-1

This book was typeset in Modern Appliances, Founders Grotesk, Al kelso and Super Grotesk OT.
The illustrations were created and coloured digitally.

Edited by Joanna McInerney
Designed by Winsome d'Abreu
Production by Ché Creasey and Nick Read

Printed in China

FSC www.fsc.org MIX Paper from responsible sources FSC® C104723

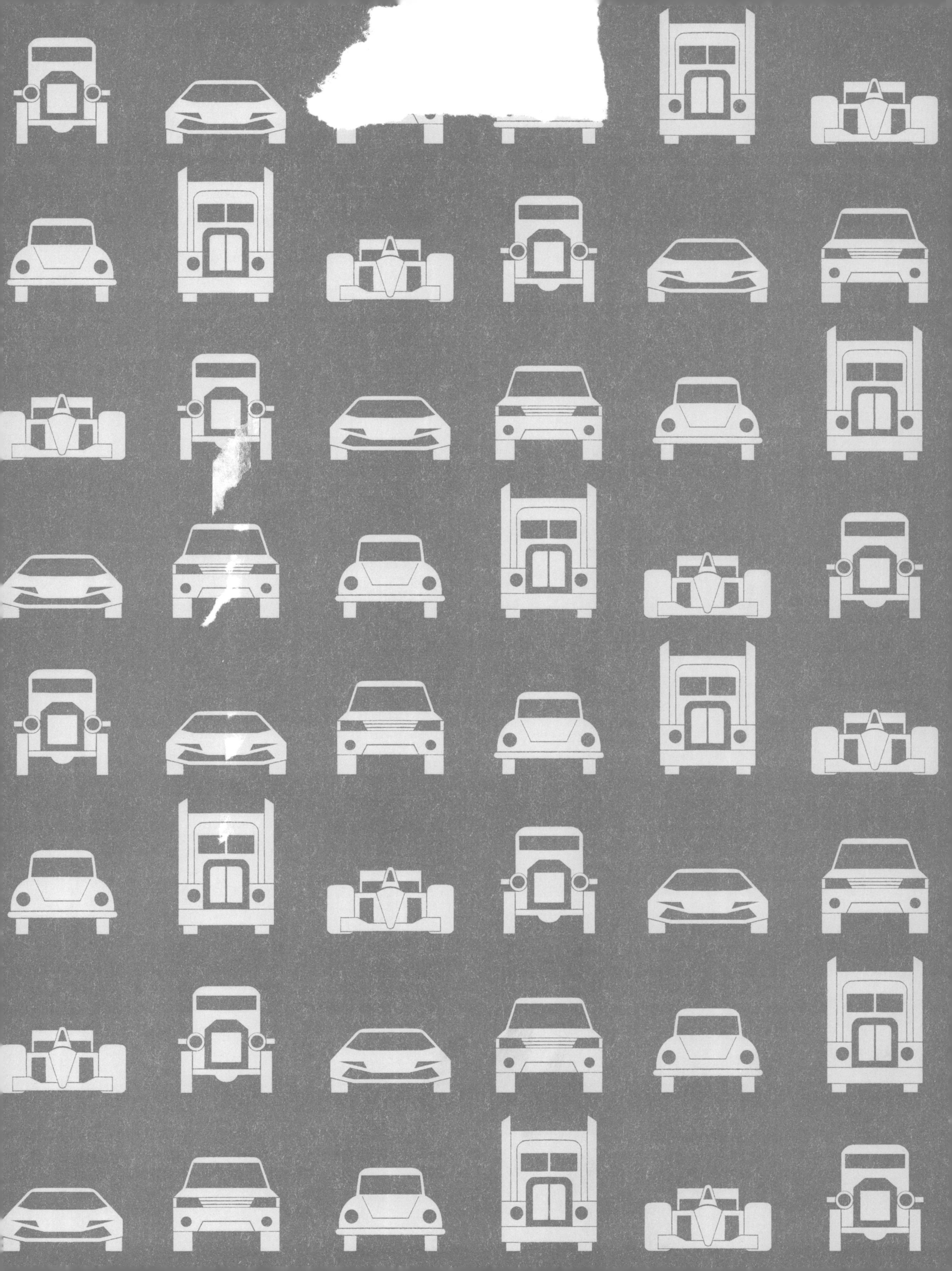

MATT RALPHS

RYO TAKEMASA

AUTOMOTIVE

BPP

CONTENTS

INTRODUCTION

There aren't many technological inventions that have changed our world so much and so quickly as the automobile. The car has given ordinary people more freedom than any other vehicle in history. With a car, we can travel anywhere we want – even journeys thousands of miles long – whenever we want. Just think: with a top speed of around 60km/h, the fastest method of private transport available before the first automobiles hit the road in the late 1800s was the two-wheeled chariot – invented over 4,000 years ago.

As well as providing speed and the ability to cover long distances, the automobile is also affordable. When horses were the main mode of private transport, only the wealthy could afford to keep them, leaving most people to either jolt along on a cart, or simply walk. This meant that ordinary people rarely travelled far from home (although the advent of the railways in the early 1800s did widen their horizons). Mass production of cheaper cars in the 1920s opened up the world to anyone with a decent-paying job.

Automobiles are convenient too. Horses need constant attention: they must be fed, watered and exercised every day, and they can only travel so far before they need a rest. As well as being able to carry more people (plus luggage), a well-maintained car can sit patiently on the drive or in the garage until needed. And all it takes to start it up is the turn of a key or the press of a button.

Of course, not all automobiles are made simply to take us from A-to-B. Some, such as top fuel dragsters and Formula One racing cars, are designed to amaze us with their speed. Others, such as the President of the United States' 'Beast' limousine, or the M8 Greyhound armoured car, are designed to protect their occupants.

So, fasten your seatbelt and get ready to enter the age of the automobile.

STEAM AND ELECTRIC AUTOMOBILES

Since their invention in the early 1800s, steam locomotives revolutionised the way people and freight were transported. However, some travellers wanted a more convenient vehicle that they didn't have to share and could use whenever they wanted. Some engineers created small, steam-powered road vehicles, while others decided to try electric battery automobiles. Many designs were created, but by the early 20th century it was clear that the internal combustion engine was going to be king of the road.

The first steam-powered road vehicle was designed by English inventor Richard Trevithick. Using a high-pressure boiler for more power, his Puffing Devil set off with six passengers in 1801 at a speed described by one witness as 'faster than I could walk' (about 8km/h). Unfortunately, only a few days after this historic journey, the boiler caught fire and Puffing Devil was destroyed.

Electric cars were very popular in Europe and the USA from the late 1800s to the early 1900s. They were quieter and smoother, didn't produce smoke and were easier to use than steam-powered automobiles. One of the first successful models was the Flocken Elektrowagen. Designed in Germany in 1888, its 1hp electric motor drove the back wheels and could reach around 15km/h.

One of the last and most advanced steam automobiles was the Doble steam car. Designed in 1924, the Doble Model E only required 30 seconds to boil the water needed to drive the engine, was easy to control and could reach speeds as high as 120km/h.

EARLY ENGINES

The age of the automobile really began with the invention of the internal combustion engine. When fuels such as petrol, diesel or kerosene are burned (or 'combusted') inside the engine (using an oxydizer such as air), they produce kinetic energy, which makes the vehicle move. Internal combustion engines are more fuel-efficient than steam engines, and proved far easier and more convenient to start-up, operate and maintain.

German inventor Karl Benz developed the first automobile powered by an internal combustion engine in 1885. His revolutionary Motorwagen had a 3hp petrol engine, three-spoked wheels with solid rubber tyres and one forward gear. Its top speed was around 16km/h.

The first mass-produced car was the Oldsmobile Model R Curved Dash; 19,000 were built between 1901 and 1907. It was more affordable than most other cars at the time, had a 5hp engine, 2 forward and 1 reverse gear and came as either a 2-seater 'runabout' or a 4-seater family car.

Created in 1901 by German engineers Paul Daimler and Wilhelm Maybach as a racing car, the Mercedes 35 HP was a huge step forward in automobile design. It had a powerful petrol engine mounted at the front that drove the back wheels, a hand brake and a foot brake, 4 forward gears and 1 reverse gear.

- FAMOUS RACES -

MONTE CARLO RALLY

The Monte Carlo Rally is one of the most exciting and unpredictable automobile races in the world. It is also one of the oldest. It began when Albert I, Prince of Monaco, asked the Automobile Club de Monaco to plan a brand-new racing event to encourage tourists to his sunny city-state on the south coast of France. His idea was for drivers to start the race from various locations all over Europe and meet – or 'rally' – at Monte Carlo.

Twenty-three drivers took up the challenge, and the first Monte Carlo Rally began in the depths of winter in January 1911. Starting from different European cities, including Berlin, Brussels and Paris, competitors had to cope with driving at night, in wind, rain and snow, and with normal traffic still running alongside them. These were long, arduous journeys that were tough on drivers as well as their machines. Strangely,

winners of the earliest Monte Carlo Rallies were not decided solely on how quickly they covered the journey. They were also judged on how comfortable the car was for the passengers and **mechanics** onboard, and its overall appearance and technical state when it crossed the finish line.

These days around 75 professional drivers (and their co-drivers) take part in the Monte Carlo Rally, driving nimble yet powerful cars from manufacturers including Toyota, Citroën, Škoda, Ford, Renault, Peugeot and Volkswagen. Although the cars are safer and more reliable than they were, the drivers still face similar dangers, including **hairpin bends** on mountain passes, roads covered in snow and ice, and unprotected spectators lining the routes. There really is nothing like the famous Monte Carlo Rally.

TYPES OF CAR

Automobiles share many design features: they all have four wheels, doors, an engine, and are operated by a single driver. However, they are also an extremely versatile form of transport, and there are many different types – spacious ones for families, all-terrain ones for adventurers – to suit people's differing needs.

Saloons (also called 'sedans' or 'four-door cars') have a boot lid that's hinged below the rear window. This keeps luggage completely separate from the passenger compartment. They are usually longer than hatchbacks. 'Saloon' comes from the French word *salon*, which means 'large room'.

Hatchbacks (also called 'three-' or 'five-door' cars) are popular with families. They're usually smaller than saloons, and have a full-height boot lid that hinges from the roof and includes the rear window.

SUVs (or 'sports utility vehicles') can seat up to seven people. They're usually four-wheel drive, which means power from the engine is sent to all four wheels. SUVs also have high **suspension** to provide extra ground clearance, and are designed to drive comfortably over rough terrain.

Coupes are sportier than a saloon. They usually have a fixed roof (unlike a convertible), a rear that slopes down, two doors, and seats for four people. 'Coupe' comes from the French word *couper*, which means 'cut', reflecting the idea that this car type is a shorter, or 'cut down', version of a more standard design.

Sports cars are not designed to be practical – they're designed to be fast and fun to drive. The first sports cars appeared in the early 1900s and the style has been popular ever since. They usually seat two people, ride low to the ground and their rear-wheel-driving engines are placed near the back to improve **traction** and **acceleration**.

Convertibles (also called 'cabriolets' or 'soft tops') are cars of any type with roofs that can be folded down to give the driver and passengers an open-air experience – perfect for summertime drives in warm weather. Most convertible roofs have a hinged metal framework covered in flexible material that folds either manually or automatically.

– FAMOUS RACES –

RALLY FINLAND

Rally Finland is such a fast race that drivers call it the Gravel Grand Prix. Souped-up road cars slide and slalom through the woods of Finland at an average speed of around 130km/h, taking high-velocity turns and jumping (known as 'hill-topping' or 'yumping') over blind crests in the road. The longest 'yump' was taken in 2003 when Markko Märtin took off for 57m at 171km/h in his Ford Focus RS WRC. That's about the length of six double-decker buses.

Rallying is an intense test of human and machine. Drivers compete by racing as fast as they can along multiple sections (or 'stages') of closed-off public roads, which can be covered in gravel, mud, dirt, snow and ice. The dangers they face include hairpin bends, ditches, water obstacles such as fords, and rough and slippery surfaces. Rally cars are specially adapted road-legal automobiles. To reduce weight, every non-essential item is stripped out. The **chassis** is strengthened. Heavy-duty suspension and

powerful brakes are added. Safety is a priority; steel **roll cages** are welded to the bodyshell to prevent roof collapses, and drivers are further protected by special racing seats, harnesses, helmets and fire extinguishers.

Victory is not won by speed alone. Teamwork between the driver and co-driver is essential. It is the co-driver's job to tell the driver exactly what lies ahead: jumps, obstacles, the direction and sharpness of upcoming turns and the best position to be on the road. They do this by reading from their 'pacenotes', which are detailed descriptions of the whole track. This constant stream of vital information allows the driver to completely concentrate on driving. Co-drivers also have to deal with the maintenance, repairs and tyre changes needed during the rough and tumble of a rally.

MASS PRODUCTION

Most of the millions of cars built every year are mass produced in heavily automated factories. Production starts with the chassis, which moves along the production lines as stationary robots attach components to it, as if completing a giant 3D jigsaw puzzle, until a finished, ready-to-drive car rolls out of the factory doors.

The first moving assembly line was invented by American automobile manufacturer Henry Ford in 1913. Workers had one task – such as attaching a wheel or a door – which they repeated over and over as each unfinished Ford Model T rolled past. Ford's industry-changing innovation reduced the time it took to make a car from 12 hours to an incredible one-and-a-half.

1) The chassis is the frame on which all the other automobile components are attached. It has to be strong to support heavy elements such as the engine, durable to last many years and also lightweight enough so the car runs efficiently.

4) The dashboard is fitted. This contains various controls as well as dials that give the driver vital information (such as speed and fuel or batteryl levels). Modern dashboards are designed to be user-friendly.

7) Most cars have four wheels. Two wheels (usually the rear pair) are attached to the engine – these are the 'driving' wheels (although some cars are four-wheel drive). The front wheels are attached to the steering wheel.

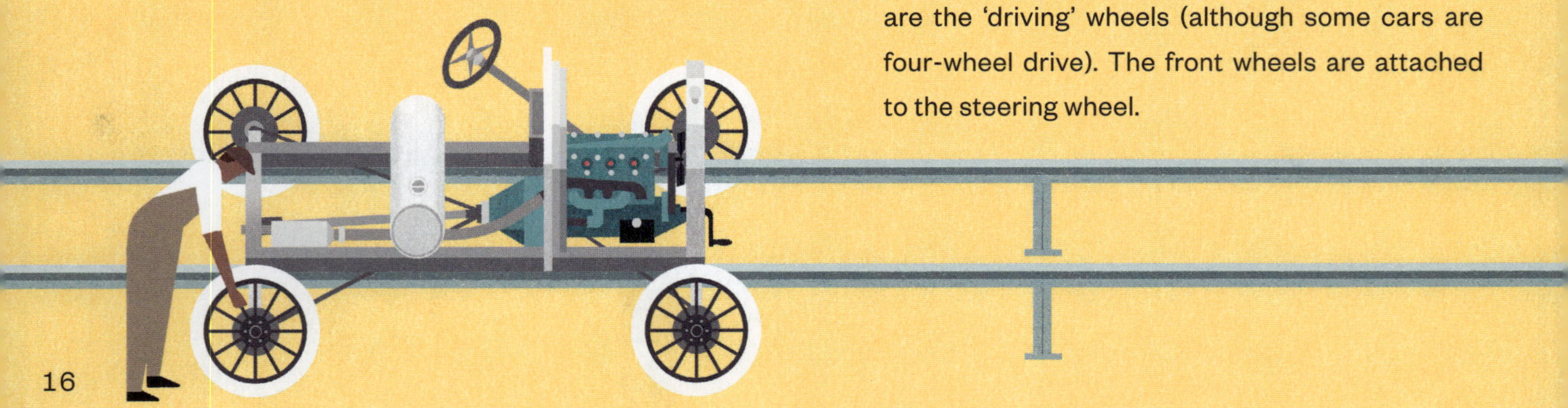

2) The petrol tank is added next. This stores the fuel needed to make the car run. Modern cars with internal combustion engines (including hybrid cars, which are also powered by electricity) use petrol, diesel or biofuels. Pure electric cars have batteries instead of tanks.

3) One of the heaviest and most complex components, the engine provides the kinetic energy needed to drive along the road. In Ford's factories it was lowered into place with a crane suspended over the moving assembly line.

5) Located underneath and towards the back of the car, the muffler (also called a 'silencer') is an important part of the exhaust system. Its main job is to reduce the noise that the engine makes.

6) Engines create heat, and if it's allowed to build up it can seriously damage the car. The radiator stops this from happening. It contains a fluid 'coolant' that circulates through a series of pipes, drawing heat away from the engine.

8) The last section to be placed over the chassis, engine and dashboard is the body shell. This includes the roof, windows, doors, bonnet (or 'hood'), and provides protection from the wind, rain, and possible accidents and collisions.

SAFETY FIRST

A tragic piece of history was made in 1869 when an Irish woman called Mary Ward became the first person killed by an automobile. While riding in an experimental open-top, steam-driven car, she fell out and was killed. Since then, designers have tried to make cars safer and easier to drive. Here are just some of the safety features found on modern automobiles.

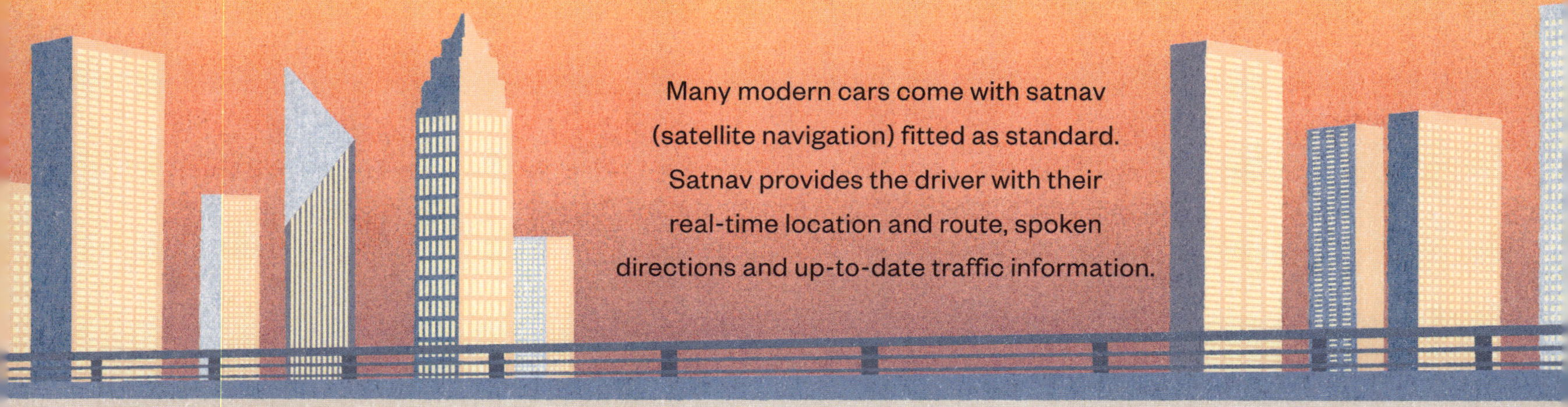

Many modern cars come with satnav (satellite navigation) fitted as standard. Satnav provides the driver with their real-time location and route, spoken directions and up-to-date traffic information.

When adaptive headlights sense a car approaching from the opposite direction they automatically dip their beams to avoid blinding the driver. They also move to follow upcoming bends in the road.

Sensors in the front of the car monitor the path ahead. If they detect an obstacle, such as a suddenly braking vehicle or a **pedestrian** stepping into the road, the automatic braking system activates and slows down the car.

Sitting in a comfortable environment allows the driver to concentrate on the road. Air conditioning controls the temperature, and heated seats add extra luxury.

Anti-lock brakes stop the wheels from locking up and skidding if the driver puts on the brakes too forcefully. Traction control ensures power is distributed evenly between the wheels, which helps the car maintain its grip even on wet or icy roads.

Seatbelts are an essential safety feature that prevents drivers and passengers from being thrown forwards should their car come to a sudden stop. They were first included as a standard feature in the Saab GT 750 in 1958.

LUXURY AUTOMOBILES

Luxury cars are designed to turn heads. They are big, heavy and sleek. Their engines purr, their paintwork and chrome shines. Passengers relax in comfortable seats, feeling barely a bump as their limousine glides down the road. From their invention in the late 1800s, automobiles have been seen as status symbols, and it wasn't long before car manufacturers realised there was money to be made by designing extra-special cars for rich people who wanted to show off their wealth.

Automobiles were not always reliable in the early 20th century. However, the cutting-edge technology (for the time) Rolls-Royce used, and the no-expense-spared attitude to materials and labour made the Silver Ghost an instantly sought-after car, and one of the first luxury automobiles.

Most luxury automobiles have a special decoration at the front. These hood ornaments symbolise the car manufacturer and are often beautifully designed works of art.

Luxury automobiles are still popular today among the rich and famous, with some of the best-known brands including Rolls-Royce, Bugatti, Bentley, Mercedes-Maybach, Lexus, BMW and Hongqi. Using up-to-date technology allows modern luxury automobiles to combine comfort and safety with high speeds and acceleration.

The most extravagant modern luxury cars cost hundreds of thousands of pounds, and can include features such as fragrance systems to make the air smell nice, retractable gear sticks and hood ornaments, drinks glasses that automatically refill, interior trimmings made from granite, rotating dashboards and a 'starlight' interior roof made from fibre-optic lights.

At the outbreak of the First World War, the Silver Ghost's chassis formed the basis for an armoured car that was used by the British military.

People who could afford luxury cars could also afford chauffeurs to drive them around. Chauffeurs were responsible for keeping the car running smoothly and looking clean and polished at all times.

MOTORBIKES

Like automobiles, motorbikes are a popular form of private transport. However, the driving experience is different. Dressed in helmets and leather overalls, riders sit astride the engine and use their bodyweight to help steer as they speed down the road on two wheels.

The first petrol-powered motorcycle was invented in Germany in 1885. The Reitwagen ('riding car') had a wooden frame, two wheels (plus two small 'stabilizers'), a crank-started engine and a top speed of 11km/h. Although never mass produced, the Reitwagen inspired other engineers to create their own designs.

During the First World War, the Allies wanted a fast, agile vehicle that could cope with rough terrain. Tens of thousands of motorbikes like this 16hp Indian Powerplus were manufactured for the war effort. Their task was to scout enemy movements, transport wounded soldiers and carry messages quickly.

Not all motorbikes are superfast. In fact, the most produced motorbike in history (around 60 million units) has a top speed of only 70km/h. Cheap and reliable, the Honda Super Cub has been in production since 1958. Small motorbikes, mopeds and scooters are perfect for driving through busy city streets.

Touring motorbikes like this Honda Gold Wing are built for people who want to enjoy long journeys (or 'tours'). As well as big fuel tanks and luggage **panniers**, these 'full-dress' tourers are built for comfort and have windshields, soft saddles and a relaxed, upright seat position.

Dirt bikes like this Yamaha YZ125 are for off-road adventures. With their lightweight frames, exaggerated suspension, high ground clearance and heavy-duty tyres, dirt bikes are designed to traverse mud, sand or dirt, and handle jumps, ditches and treacherous paths with ease.

As technology has advanced, engineers have created ever more sophisticated motorbikes. Sports bikes like this Kawasaki Ninja ZX-6R (top speed 260km/h) are all about acceleration and speed on **straights**, and control and handling around corners. Modified sports bikes used in racing are called 'superbikes'.

– FAMOUS RACES –

ISLE OF MAN TOURIST TROPHY

Every summer, the Isle of Man hosts one of the most amazing, and exceptionally dangerous, motorsport events in the world: the Tourist Trophy, better known simply as the 'TT'. Unlike other motorbike races, the TT runs entirely on closed-off public roads, and riders from all over the world take their lives in their hands to speed, swoop and swerve their superfast vehicles around the famous 60.72km-long Mountain Course.

The TT has changed a lot since it started in 1907, with different routes and motorbike types used over the years. These days, the first week is given over to practice sessions and time trials, and the second to the actual races. Thrill-seeking spectators line the roads as motorbikes streak past, reaching well over 200km/h, their

riders using all their skill to gain the quickest lap time. And there is a world of difference between travelling speeds like that around a dedicated racing track to the natural **contours**, dips and rises found on the Isle of Man. Riders must negotiate narrow, twisting roads lined with buildings, walls, ditches and trees. This demands steel nerves and unwavering concentration. One mistake, one misjudged jump, one poorly timed turn can lead to serious injury – or worse. Since 1907, there have been around 260 riders killed. For competitors this danger is a vital part of the TT experience, allowing them to become part of an elite group, brave enough to take on the toughest motorbike race in the world. However, recent changes – including reducing the number of competitors, introducing better safety equipment and warm-up laps before the race – have made the event safer.

THE DAYTONA 500

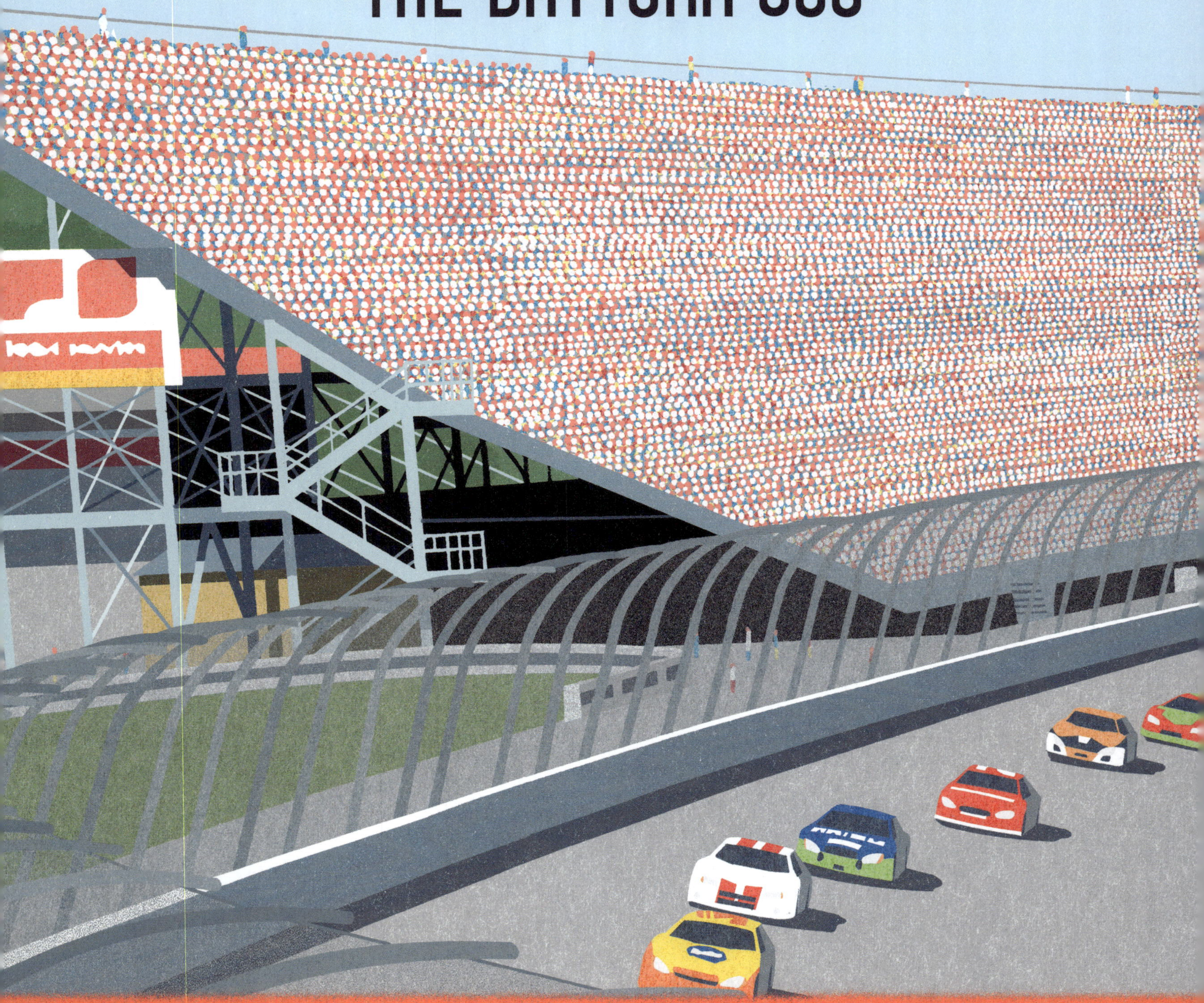

Also called 'The Great American Race', the Daytona 500 is the most famous event in the annual NASCAR Cup Series. Named after its 500-mi (800-km) length, the Daytona 500 sees around 40 stock cars (two cars per team) race bumper-to-bumper and door-to-door, 200 times around the Daytona International Speedway: a 4km-long track with steeply banked corners and long straights. Cars often remain bunched together throughout the entire 3.5-hour race, meaning last-minute overtakes to secure a win are always thrillingly possible.

NASCAR stands for the National Association for Stock Car Auto Racing. Stock car racing's roots can be traced back to the American Prohibition, a period between 1920 and 1933 when it was illegal to produce, transport

and sell alcohol in the USA. Smugglers, known as 'bootleggers', modified their cars in order to outrun the police. When Prohibition ended, these excitement-seeking drivers decided to race their souped-up cars on the sands of Daytona Beach – and stock car racing was born. The first official NASCAR race took place in 1949, and the competing cars were a wide variety of ordinary, unmodified factory models.

Over the following years, more and more modifications to increase safety and improve car performance were permitted, and modern NASCAR vehicles, with their roll cages, hand-built **aerodynamic** bodyshells, highly tuned engines (capable of average race speeds of 300km/h) are a world away from the ordinary street cars that bumped and slewed over the sands of Daytona Beach all those decades ago.

CONCEPT CARS

Automobile manufacturers constantly strive to make technological breakthroughs and futuristic car designs. Most ideas are so outlandish, experimental or potentially expensive they never get beyond the planning stage. But some are considered worth the time and expense to turn into concept cars. Also called 'prototypes', concept cars are presented at motor shows to gauge public reaction. If the response is positive, the manufacturer may decide to turn their concept into a mass-produced car.

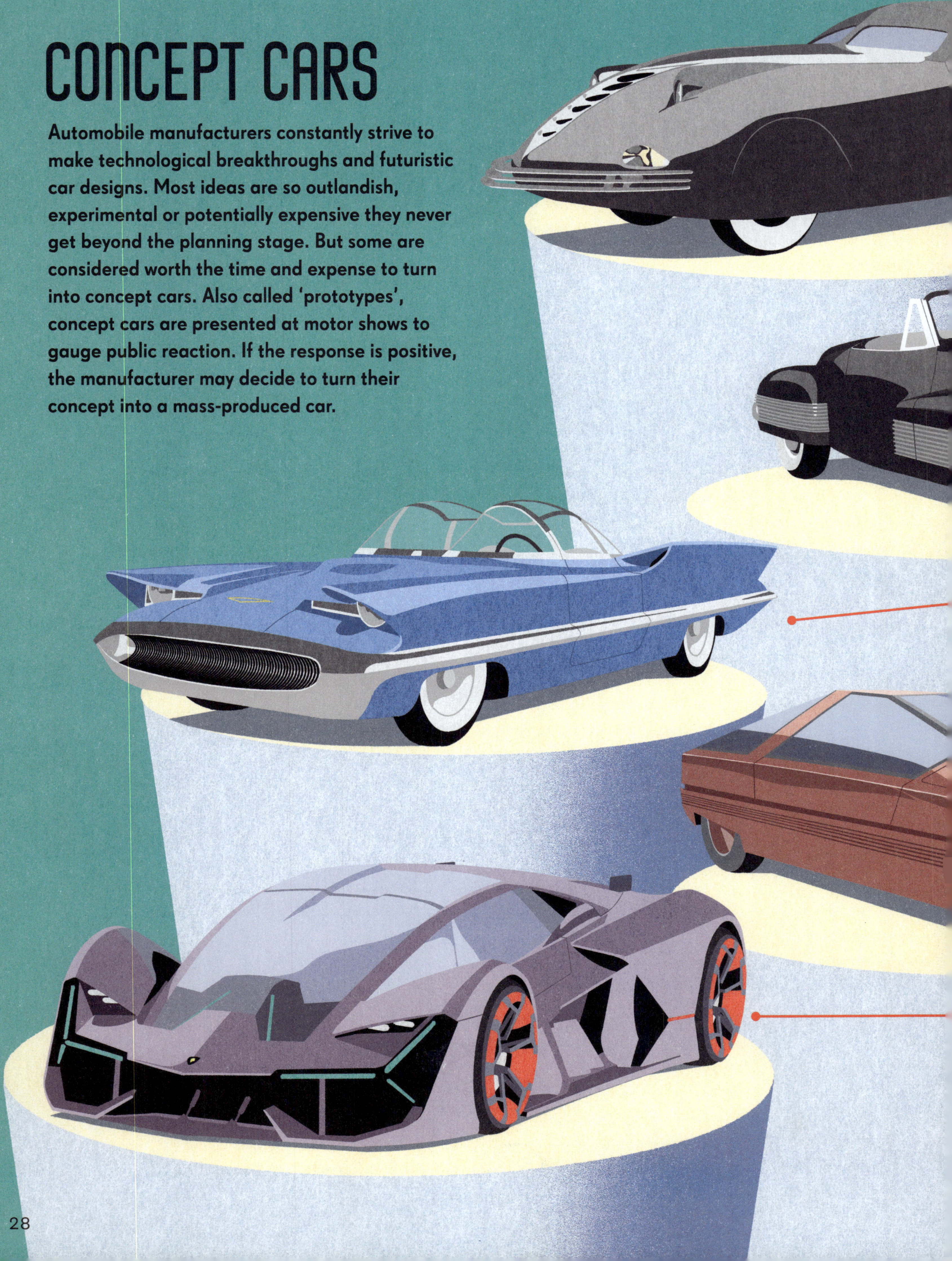

The Phantom Corsair is a one-of-a-kind vehicle designed by an American engineer called Rust Heinz. This aerodynamic, two-ton luxury supercar seated six people (four up front, two in back), featured 'enveloped' wheels, push-button automatic doors, green-tinted safety glass, and had a top speed of 115km/h. Sadly, Heinz was killed aged 24 in a car crash in 1939, and his dream of manufacturing the Corsair for sale died with him.

Built in 1938, the Buick Y-Job was the first concept car. Showing off many new style ideas, it was envisioned by designer Harley Earl. This sleek, low-riding, two-seater convertible had a 5.2l 'straight-8' engine, wrap-around bumpers, hidden headlights and electric roof and windows. Although the Y-Job was never mass-produced, American manufacturers were greatly influenced by its stylish design.

The Lincoln Futura was revealed in 1955. Designed in the USA and hand-built in Italy, this long, low, aerodynamic coupe featured a double canopy, hooded headlights, dramatic **tailfins**, and cost the equivalent of £1.7 million in today's money. Never mass-produced, it did however influence other Lincoln cars, and was used as the basis for the Batmobile in the 1960's TV series *Batman*.

The Citroën Karin is one of the oddest concept cars ever shown. Appearing in 1980, the Karin had two **butterfly doors** and was pyramid-shaped, with most of the top half dominated by huge windows; the roof was only about the size of a piece of A3 paper. One of its most unusual features was the three-seat layout with the driver sitting in the middle.

As the world slowly moves away from **fossil fuel**-burning vehicles, more prototypes are appearing that showcase the advances being made in electric cars. The experimental Lamborghini Terzo Millennio (which means 'third millennium') is an electric coupe that uses fast-recharging **supercapacitors** instead of batteries. Each wheel (which glows orange for a futuristic look) has its own e-motor and the carbon fibre bodyshell is highly aerodynamic.

THE FASTEST CARS

From the automobile's invention in the late 1800s, engineers have competed to build the fastest cars on the planet. The World Land Speed Record is won by driving the fastest average speed (from two runs) in a wheeled land vehicle over a 1.6-km distance. Attempts are usually made over deserts and salt flats because the ground is hard, flat and there are no obstacles to crash into.

In 1927, the Sunbeam 1,000-hp became the first automobile to travel at 328km/h. Wrestling with the power generated by twin V12 Matabele aircraft engines, British driver Henry Segrave had to drive Sunbeam into the sea at Daytona Beach to slow down after the wind caused him to swerve and nearly lose control.

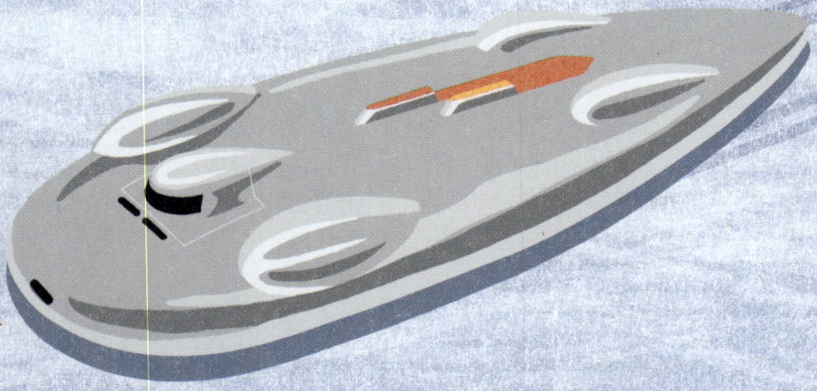

Silver, streamlined and sleek, the Railton Special looks like something from a science fiction film. In 1939, this 3-ton, 8.4m-long automobile powered by two supercharged Napier Lion W12 aeroplane engines, reached 595km/h on the Bonneville Salt Flats in the USA. The Railton Special and British driver John Cobb held the record for another 25 years.

Cobb's record was eventually broken in 1964 by British speed legend Donald Campbell when he pushed his 4,000hp Bristol Proteus gas turbine-powered Bluebird CN7 to 649km/h. Unfortunately, the racing surface of Lake Eyre in Australia was not completely dry; if it had been, it's likely Bluebird would have gone even faster.

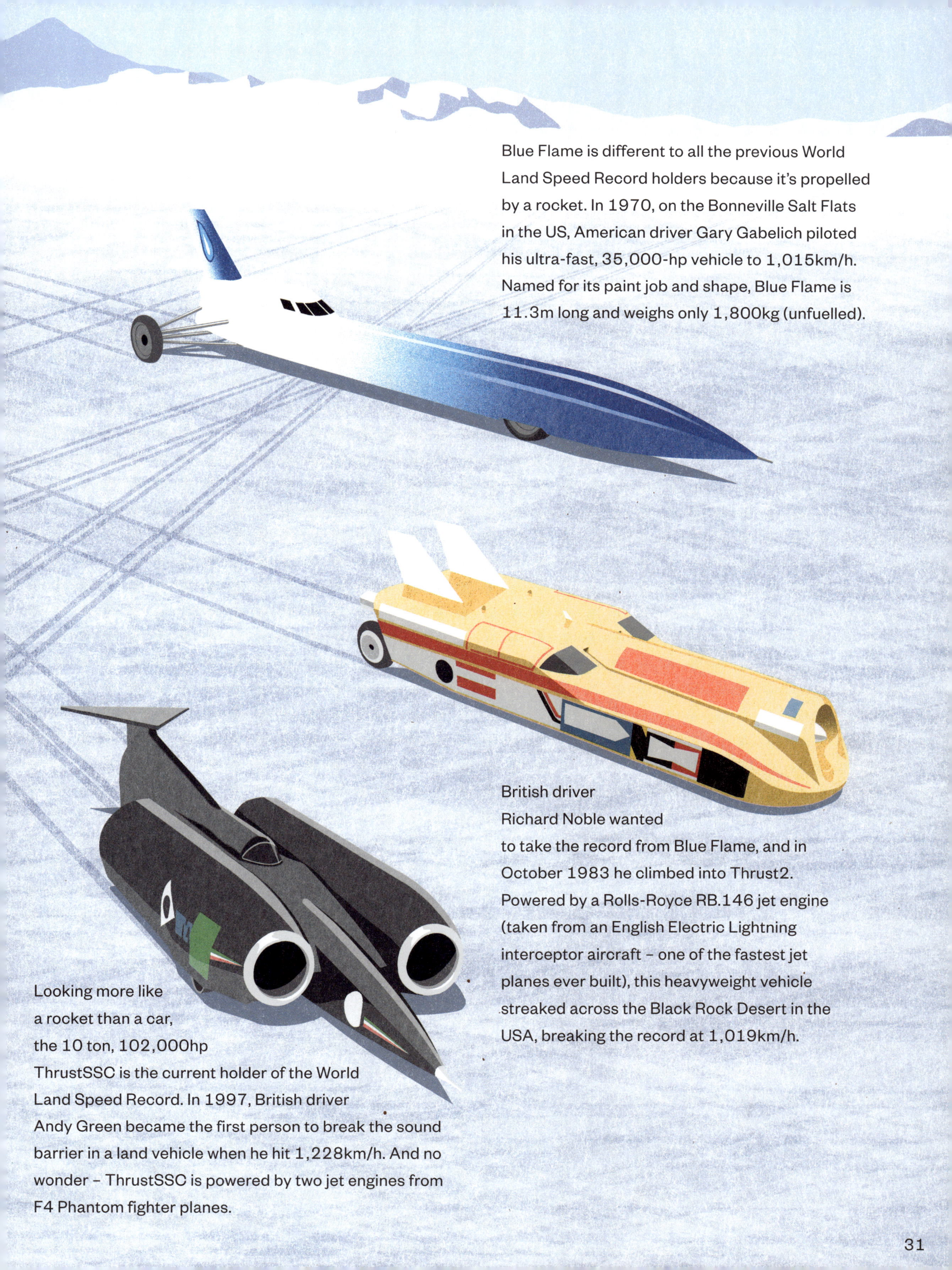

Blue Flame is different to all the previous World Land Speed Record holders because it's propelled by a rocket. In 1970, on the Bonneville Salt Flats in the US, American driver Gary Gabelich piloted his ultra-fast, 35,000-hp vehicle to 1,015km/h. Named for its paint job and shape, Blue Flame is 11.3m long and weighs only 1,800kg (unfuelled).

British driver Richard Noble wanted to take the record from Blue Flame, and in October 1983 he climbed into Thrust2. Powered by a Rolls-Royce RB.146 jet engine (taken from an English Electric Lightning interceptor aircraft – one of the fastest jet planes ever built), this heavyweight vehicle streaked across the Black Rock Desert in the USA, breaking the record at 1,019km/h.

Looking more like a rocket than a car, the 10 ton, 102,000hp ThrustSSC is the current holder of the World Land Speed Record. In 1997, British driver Andy Green became the first person to break the sound barrier in a land vehicle when he hit 1,228km/h. And no wonder – ThrustSSC is powered by two jet engines from F4 Phantom fighter planes.

FORMULA ONE

Formula One is the fastest motorsport in the world. Every year, expert drivers in their speed-machines compete on tracks all over the globe to become World Champion. There is hardly a more exciting sight than seeing the most technically advanced racing cars line up on the starting grid, engines roaring, as they wait for the lights to go out. Here are just some of the iconic cars and drivers from Formula One's 70-year history.

Argentinian Juan Manuel Fangio was there at the start of Formula One. He dominated the 1950s by winning the Driver's Championship five times, driving for four different teams, and winning 24 of the 52 races he entered. Victory came at a cost, and in 1952 he was thrown from his car and suffered a broken neck. However, Fangio was back racing in the next season.

Scottish Jim Clark didn't just drive in Formula One, he also successfully competed in sports car tournaments as well as the famous Le Mans 24-hour race and the Indianapolis 500. Driving with Lotus, Clark won two world championships (in 1963 and 1965) and won 25 of the 72 races he entered. Sadly he died at the age of 32 when he crashed during a Formula Two race in Germany.

Austrian driver Niki Lauda is famous for many things: his fierce rivalry with British racer James Hunt, winning the World Championship three times, and the terrible accident that nearly ended his career, and his life. In 1976 Lauda crashed his Ferrari 312T, inhaled toxic gasses and suffered severe burns to his face. Somehow he survived, and went on to lose that year's Championship by *only one point.*

Who can say how much more success the brilliant Brazilian Ayrton Senna would have had if he'd not been killed aged 34 in a crash while leading the pack in the 1994 San Marino Grand Prix. Spending most of his career racing for McLaren, Senna won three World Championships and 41 Grand Prix out of 161. Few other drivers can match the passion and skill he brought to the racetrack.

German Michael Schumacher had the elements needed to become a successful Formula One driver: quick reflexes, physical fitness, mental toughness, bravery, intelligence, ruthlessness, as well as the ability to push his car and himself to the limit. The numbers are staggering: seven world championships, 91 wins from a total of 306 races, 68 pole position starts, 77 fastest-lap records and a career that lasted 30 years.

British driver Lewis Hamilton says he was inspired as a boy when he watched Ayrton Senna race. He's come a long way since then and broken many records with Mercedes: so far he's won seven World Championship titles (level with Schumacher), 103 of his 288 Grand Prix, 103 pole positions and 59 fastest-lap records.

– FAMOUS RACES –

MONACO GRAND PRIX

The Monaco Grand Prix is one of the most unusual races in Formula One. Instead of speeding around a specially designed race track, drivers must negotiate the hills, narrow streets and extremely tight corners of the city-state of Monaco. Because this Grand Prix is so difficult and demanding, it is 45km shorter (at 260km) than all the others in the season. Another challenge unique to Monaco is the tunnel; darker than the rest of the track, the light change can affect the driver's eyesight.

Formula One has enthralled its fans since the first driver's world championship began at Silverstone race track in the UK in 1950. A modern Formula One racing season features 10 teams (including Mercedes, Ferrari, McLaren and Williams), 20 drivers (two per team) and about 22 tracks. The length of a Grand Prix

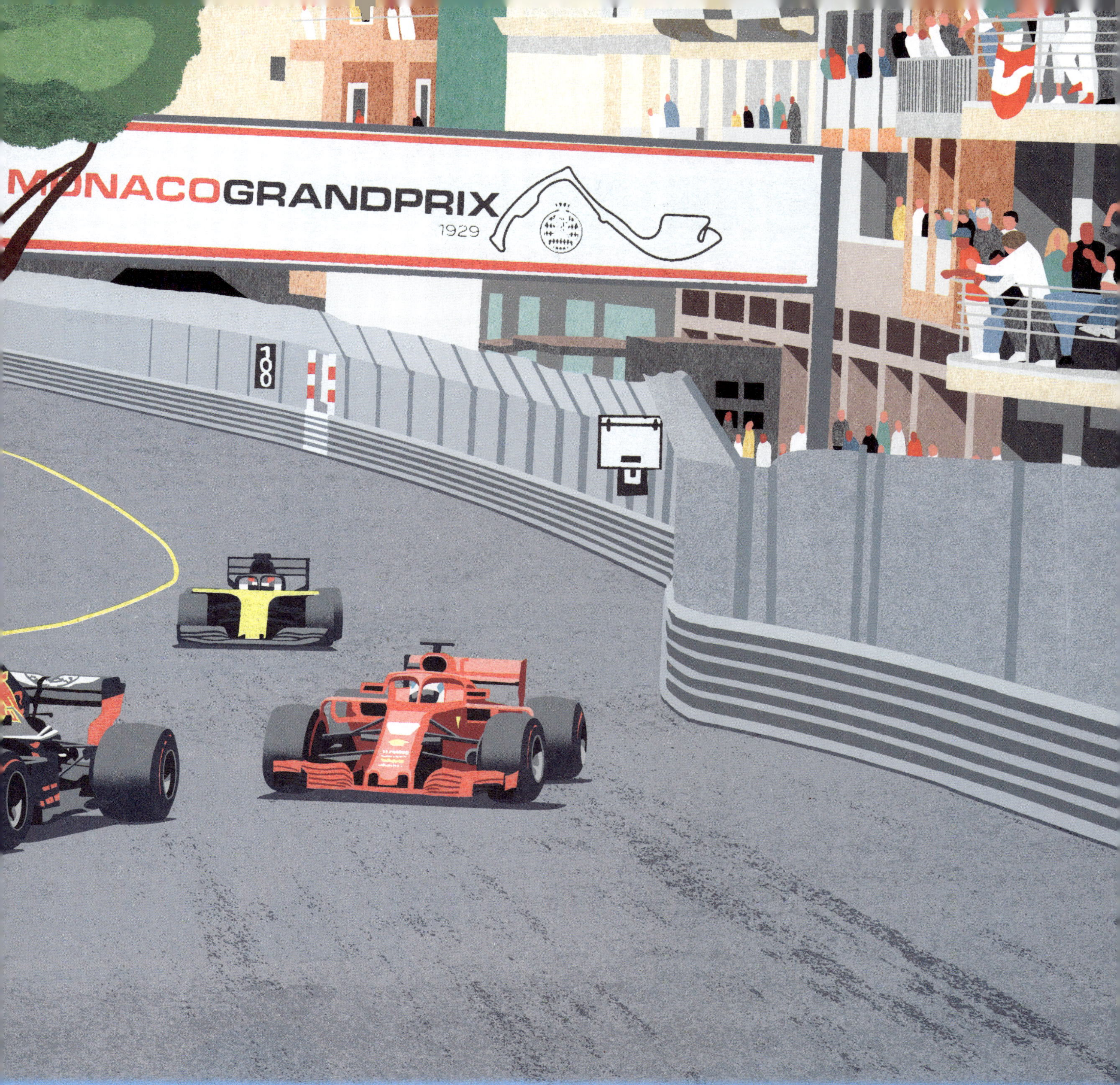

(excluding Monaco) is however many laps it takes to complete 305km. Racing weekends occur every fortnight and include a qualifying session to determine each driver's starting position. After a 'formation lap' to warm up their tyres, drivers line up on the grid, wait for the red lights on the starting board to go out and begin the race. Teams and drivers communicate with radios, but colour-coded flags waved by safety marshalls are used to provide messages and instructions to competitors: a yellow flag warns of danger ahead and tells the driver to slow down; a green flag says the danger has passed and the driver can speed up again; a red flag means the race has been stopped due to an accident or poor track conditions, and the famous chequered flag greets drivers as they cross the finish line. Tyres are also colour-coded, depending on their hardness: soft tyres are quicker and have better grip than hard tyres, but don't last as long; full wet tyres are used when the track is **waterlogged**.

ICONIC ROAD BRIDGES

Just as with roads and highways, the invention of the automobile meant new bridges and tunnels were needed. Road tunnels were bored into mountains, and road bridges constructed over ravines, valleys, gorges, rivers and lakes to allow drivers to get to where they needed to go.

The Millau Viaduct spans the scenic valley of the river Tarn in France. With its pylons towering 343m (about 20m taller than the Eiffel Tower) above the fields below, this cable-stayed road bridge is the tallest in the world.

The Golden Gate Bridge connects San Fransisco to Marin County in the USA and is one of the most famous bridges in the world. A 2.7km-long suspension bridge, it was finished in 1937 after seven years' work and painted International Orange to make it more visible to ships in fog.

Completed in 1932 after eight years using 53,000 tons of steel and 6 million rivets, the steel-arch Sydney Harbour Bridge in Australia is one of the most famous landmarks in the world. It's 503m span includes a motorway, four train tracks and pedestrian and bicycle lanes.

Constructed to ease **congestion**, the Bang Na Expressway in Thailand is the longest road bridge in the world. Completed in 2000 after five years, this box-girder bridge is 55km long, carries six lanes of traffic and needed 1.8 million m^3 of concrete to build.

At 24.5km, the Laerdal Tunnel in Norway is the longest road tunnel in the world. During the five-year construction time, 2.5 million m^3 of rock had to be excavated. The tunnel includes three beautifully lit chambers to prevent drivers getting bored and losing concentration.

TRUCKS

With their grumbling diesel engines and 18 heavy-duty wheels, trucks are the workhorses of the road. There's nothing they can't haul: from food to furniture, petrol to paper, tree trunks to televisions. Without trucks and the people who drive them, our factories wouldn't function, our shops would be empty and our deliveries wouldn't be made.

People quickly realised how useful a freight vehicle powered by an internal combustion engine would be, and in 1895 a German mechanical engineer called Karl Benz invented the first truck (he was also the inventor of the first car - see page 9). Rolling on four iron wheels and powered by a rear-mounted petrol engine, it looked like a cart without the horses. More designs followed, but it took several decades of development before trucks began to take over from the centuries-old horse and cart. These days, trucks transport billions of tons of freight every year.

The average American long-haul truck driver will spend up to 300 days per year on the road, travelling over 160,000km per year, or around 600km per day. That's a long time to sit, and many drivers customise their moving homes to make them more comfortable.

This is the Peterbilt 389. It's a Class 8 truck – the biggest available on the highways of the USA. Its long nose, which houses the engine, means it's a 'conventional' truck; flat-nosed trucks where the driver sits over the engine are called 'cab over engines' (COEs). Peterbilts are highly customisable, allowing owners to have shiny chrome exhaust pipes, air intakes, wheel hubs and front grilles, and choose from a wide variety of colours and decorative art options.

The proper name for a truck that pulls a separate trailer is actually 'tractor'. The trailer is attached to the tractor using a device called the 'fifth wheel', which is located behind the cab where the driver sits.

Long-haul truckers have a tough life, motoring along highways and motorways on journeys that can take days. Many trucks have a sleeper compartment behind the cab, complete with bed, storage space, fridge, heater and cooking facilities.

Trucks haul extremely heavy loads – sometimes several linked trailers at once – so they need powerful engines and plenty of gears (the maximum is 18 forward gears and four reverse) to keep them motoring along even up long hills.

– FAMOUS RACES –

MONSTER TRUCK SHOW

There are few more spectacularly awesome sights than a brightly painted Monster Truck bouncing and reeling around a track on four chunky wheels. Monster Truck events are showcases in scale, skill and destruction. First are the races, where drivers compete to complete laps around a circuit as fast as possible, all while crushing parked cars and leaping over ramps. Then comes the freestyle stunt competition where drivers urge their machines into jumps, spins, backflips, wheelies and doughnuts.

Monster Trucks are named well: big and powerful, these hulking machines can withstand so much damage that they often keep running even after capsizing! Modern Monster Trucks are specialised off-road vehicles powered by supercharged V8 engines that ride around 4m high on raised suspension, with virtually indestructible all-terrain tyres. Their light, fibreglass bodies are easy to remove and replace, and

can be modified into all manner of different shapes to make them look extra-striking. Safety features include engines that can be shut off remotely, and restraining straps for the most explosive and high-pressure parts of the engine.

The very first Monster Truck was created by American Bob Chandler in 1975. After years of racing his Ford F-250 4X4 pickup truck, he decided to make some major modifications to give him an edge over his rivals. Chandler increased the engine power, added four-wheel steering, raised suspension and fat 1.2m tyres. He called his creation Bigfoot®, and people flocked to see it. But Chandler wasn't finished. In 1982 he built Bigfoot 2®. Towering on enormous 1.7-m high by 1.1-m wide tyres (now standard on most Monster Trucks) it made history when it drove over and crushed two cars (now a standard Monster Truck stunt).

AMERICA

Although the automobile was invented in Europe, there are few countries where the car has had more of an impact on the landscape, culture and people's everyday lives than the USA. From the moment mass-produced cars poured from American factories, the automobile was embraced as a symbol of freedom and a gateway to opportunity.

America is vast and needs swift roads so people and cargo can travel city to city, state to state and sea to shining sea. Built between 1956 and 1992, the Interstate Highway System is around 78,000km long. Each Interstate has a one- or two-digit number (for example I-90 runs from Seattle to Boston); Interstates running east–west have even numbers, and north–south odd numbers.

Mass-produced cars and cheap fuel allowed millions of Americans in the early 20th century to fulfil their dream of riding the open road. This meant town-planners designed whole cities around the automobile rather than the pedestrian. Large areas were given over to car parks, streets were wide and laid out in grid systems and vast swathes of people moved away from the inner cities to live in suburbs.

In the early 20th century, there were hundreds of automobile manufacturers in the USA. Most were eventually swallowed by what became known as the Big Three: Ford, General Motors (GM) and Chrysler. Based in Detroit, Michigan (Detroit is nicknamed 'Motor City'), these automotive giants dominated the industry throughout much of the 20th century. Nowadays, American manufacturers face stiff competition from rivals in Japan (Toyota and Honda), Germany (Volkswagen and Daimler) and China (SAIC Motor and FAW).

Route 66 is one of the most famous highways in the world. Finished in 1926, it ran 3,940km across eight states, from Chicago, Illinois, to Los Angeles, California. Boasting breathtaking scenery and lined with motels, gas stations, diners and drive-throughs, Route 66 inspired countless musicians, film-makers and writers. Gradually replaced by Interstate Highways, Route 66 no longer officially exists, but it lives on in the American imagination.

EUROPE

During the 19th century, engineers from all over Europe contributed to the automobile's development. Many strange and wonderful self-propelled road vehicles were created: most powered by steam or electricity; some successful, some not. However, historians agree the first car was Karl Benz's 1885 'Motorwagen'. From then, Europe slowly fell in love with the automobile. Indeed, the first long distance road trip (106km) was undertaken in 1888 by Bertha Benz, Karl's fearless wife.

The European automobile industry grew during the first half of the 20th century, but at a slower rate than the American. Manufacturers lagged behind the mass-production muscle of Ford, its moving assembly lines and the tens of thousands of Model Ts it produced. Fewer cars were sold too because the average European had less money to spend than the average American. Just like America, many small manufacturers disappeared, and the market became dominated by a few automotive giants, including Austin and Morris in Britain, Renault, Peugeot and Citroën in France and Mercedes-Benz in Germany.

Europe already had a road network when the car was invented, but it was centuries old and only suitable for horses and carts. Most country roads were little more than rutted tracks, and the only paved streets were in cities. European governments realised things had to improve as more people bought cars. Finished in 1932, one of the very first motorways was 18km long and connected the German cities of Cologne and Bonn. Modern Europe is criss-crossed with thousands of kilometres of motorway, allowing free-flowing traffic to travel anywhere: from Paris to Portsmouth, Berlin to Barcelona and Lisbon to Luxembourg.

Most European towns and cities were built long before the invention of the car, and the narrow, windy streets are not ideal. Traffic jams and air pollution in built-up areas are still common problems. Methods of reducing the number of cars in city centres include Park and Ride bus services, bypasses and congestion charges.

LE MANS

The 24 Hours of Le Mans (usually shortened to Le Mans) is a motorised marathon, a ruthless test of human and machine, and the oldest endurance race in the world. Every year since 1923, around 60 cutting-edge supercars have raced continuously (apart from pit stops) for 24 hours, in all weathers and through the dead of night, around the Sarthe circuit in France. This 13.6-km route is part racetrack, part public road, and cars can reach 300km/h.

Many top automobile manufacturers including Ferrari, Aston Martin, Porsche, Ford and Jaguar have striven to produce cars with the speed, agility and sheer survivability to win glory at Le Mans. The winning car is the one that travels the furthest in 24 hours; the record, set in 2010 in an Audi R15, is 5,410.7km (397 laps) – that's nearly seven times longer than the Daytona 500 (see pages 26–27).

Each car has three drivers, who swap every two hours during a pit stop. As well as concentrating on the race, drivers must cope with dehydration, heat (Le Mans runs during summer), rainstorms (which makes the track slippery), driving in the dark and lack of sleep.

Before 1970, the race began with the so-called 'Le Mans start'. Drivers lined up opposite their cars, which were parked on the other side of the track. When the traditional French tricolour starting flag was waved, drivers sprinted to their cars, started them up and sped off. This was eventually deemed too dangerous, and now competitors begin the race from a rolling start. Unfortunately, the worst crash in motorsport history occurred at Le Mans in 1955, when a Mercedes-Benz 300 SLR hit another car, flipped, landed in the crowd and exploded, killing the driver and 83 spectators.

ROADSIDE SERVICES

As more people took to their cars and major road networks got longer, a whole host of services was developed to provide essential supplies, comfort, convenience and entertainment for drivers, especially those undertaking long-haul journeys.

Drive-through restaurants are designed for people who want to buy food quickly, conveniently and without having to get out of their cars. Customers drive up to a window and give their order directly to a server, or speak into a microphone. Then they wait for their food to be prepared and handed into the car. The first drive-through restaurant opened in the late 1940s on America's famous Route 66. It was called Red's Giant Hamburg because the owner, Sheldon 'Red' Chaney, couldn't fit the final 'er' of hamburger onto his sign!

Vehicles can't run without fuel, so it needs to be readily available at all times. Service stations (also called garages, gas, petrol and filling stations) are built by the roadside, allowing a driver to stop their vehicle by the correct pump, fill up their tank, pay and continue on with their journey. The fuel is stored in huge underground tanks, which are refilled by tanker trucks. Many service stations include grocery stores, where drivers can buy drinks, snacks, newspapers, magazines and useful items such as windscreen wiper fluid and oil for their cars.

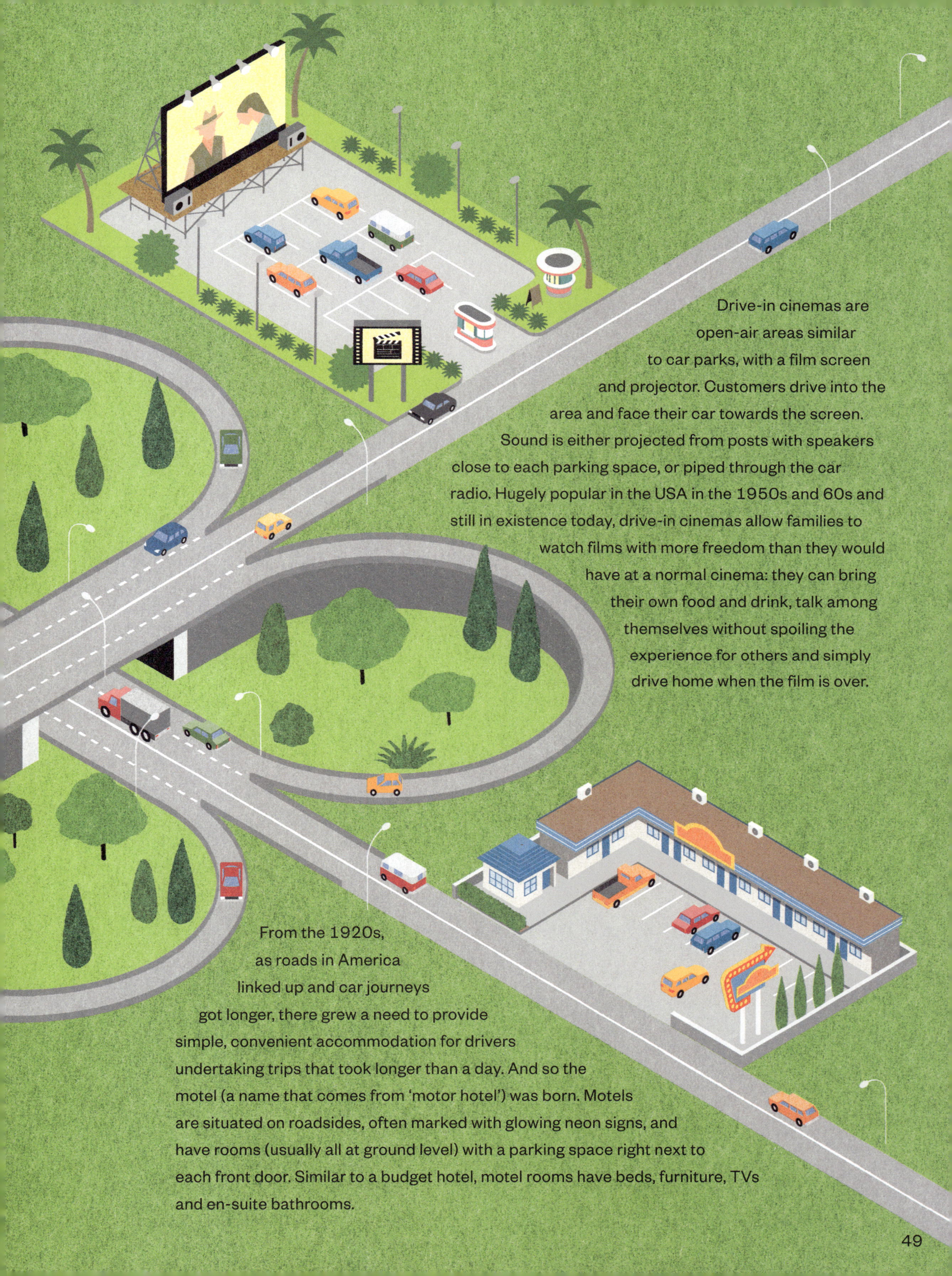

Drive-in cinemas are open-air areas similar to car parks, with a film screen and projector. Customers drive into the area and face their car towards the screen. Sound is either projected from posts with speakers close to each parking space, or piped through the car radio. Hugely popular in the USA in the 1950s and 60s and still in existence today, drive-in cinemas allow families to watch films with more freedom than they would have at a normal cinema: they can bring their own food and drink, talk among themselves without spoiling the experience for others and simply drive home when the film is over.

From the 1920s, as roads in America linked up and car journeys got longer, there grew a need to provide simple, convenient accommodation for drivers undertaking trips that took longer than a day. And so the motel (a name that comes from 'motor hotel') was born. Motels are situated on roadsides, often marked with glowing neon signs, and have rooms (usually all at ground level) with a parking space right next to each front door. Similar to a budget hotel, motel rooms have beds, furniture, TVs and en-suite bathrooms.

HOT RODS

Hot rods come in a huge variety of shapes, sizes, colours and technical specifications. That's because they're designed and built by people who want to speed down highways, dragstrips and racing tracks in something unique. Hot rods are usually American cars that have been heavily modified for maximum acceleration and speed, and sport eye-catching paint jobs that turn them into works of automotive art.

In the 1930s, many Americans loved to tinker with their Ford Model Ts to make them faster, and then race on the dry lakebeds of California. However, the idea of customising cars became really popular in the late 1940s when thousands of US servicemen returned home from the Second World War. The excellent mechanical training they'd received in the Army, Navy and Air Force meant they knew exactly how to turn ordinary cars into speed machines – and the hot rod craze began.

Hot rods like this 1932 Ford Deuce are automobiles that have been stripped down and souped-up to make them go faster. Removing bumpers, **fenders** and bonnets (exposing the engine) makes the car lighter; adding wider wheels improves traction; engines are 'tuned' to make them more powerful, or replaced with something better. Some owners 'channel' and 'chop' their hot rods to make them ride lower to the ground, which reduces wind resistance, improves **stability** and makes them look cool.

A quality paint job is one of the best ways to make a hot rod stand out. Fuelled by a desire for uniqueness, hot rod enthusiasts usually choose schemes that differ wildly from anything offered by the car manufacturers: bright and contrasting colours, transparent paints overlaid onto metallic undercoats, high-gloss or matt finishes, decorative patterns such as 'pinstripe' lines or flames, and many more.

MUSCLE CARS

Muscle cars are powerful, stylish and make a lot of noise. The first was the 1964 Pontiac GTO. Fitted with a 6.4l V8 engine, it went from 0–100km/h in only six seconds. Other American manufacturers quickly began producing their own muscle cars, including the Plymouth Superbird, Chevrolet Chevelle and the Oldsmobile 442.

The Dodge Charger first roared onto highways in 1968. A classic muscle car, this 1969 model is powered by a V8 engine and has headlight covers that flip up when the driver turns on the lights. An aerodynamic **nose cone** and a stabiliser wing were added to create the Charger 'Daytona' model, built especially for NASCAR stock racing (see pages 26–27).

Muscle cars are often used in action films. The Dodge Charger starred in one of the most famous film car chases of all time. In the 1968 American thriller *Bullitt*, a Charger is pursued by a modified Ford Mustang GT Fastback through the hilly streets of San Francisco. The 10-minute, dialogue-free scene took three weeks to film and involved jumps, screeching high-speed turns and unscripted crashes.

V8 engines that most muscle cars of the 1960s and 70s used were fuel-inefficient and produced lots of harmful **emissions**. So, when fuel prices increased and people became concerned about air pollution, muscle cars nearly died out. However, modern high-performance engines are more efficient and environmentally friendly, and so muscle cars – including new Charger and Mustang models – are back in fashion.

DRAG RACES

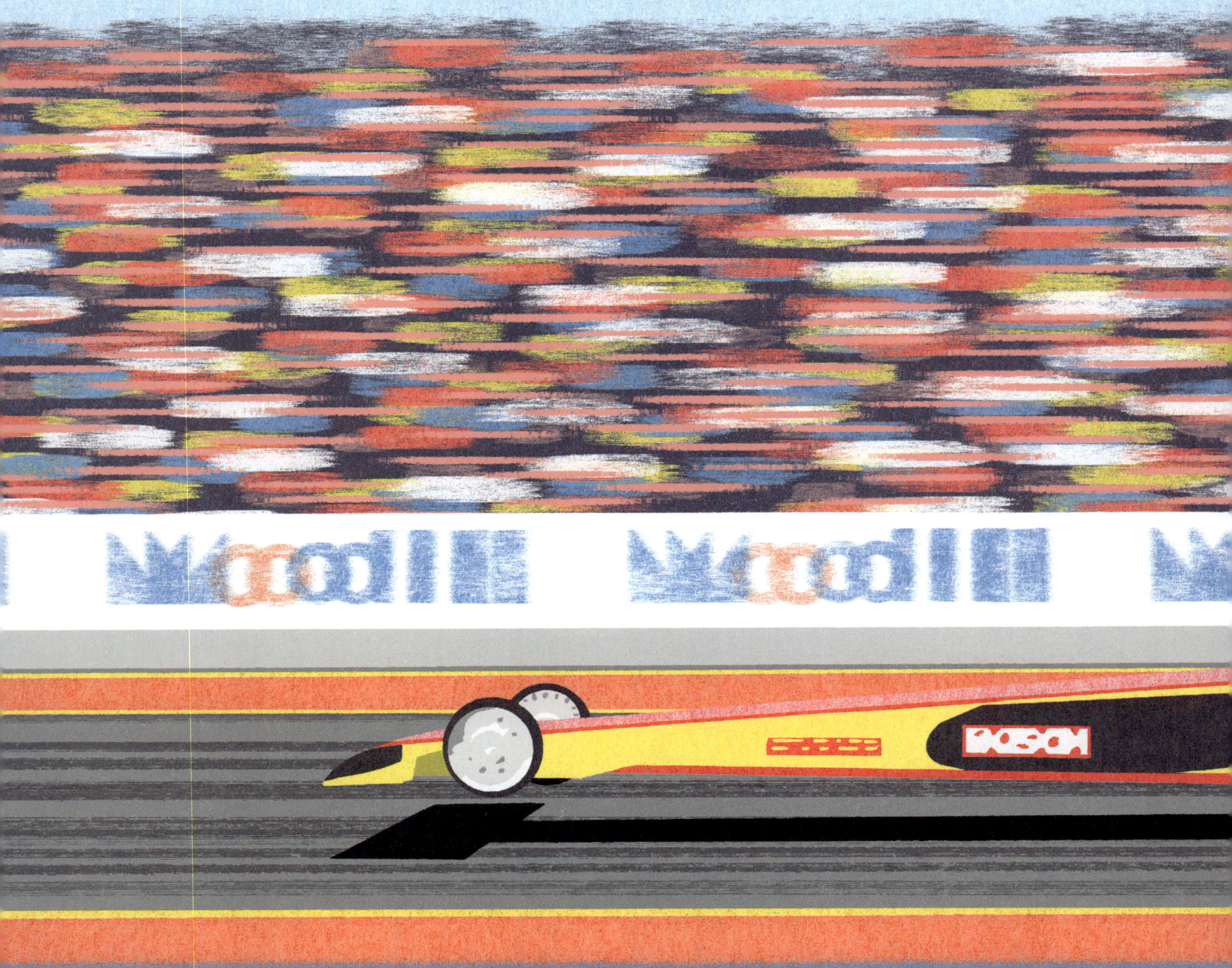

On 1 November 2019 in Las Vegas, USA, driver Brittany Force shattered the world record for the fastest speed in a Top Fuel dragster. Strapped into her 11,000hp car and shredding rubber at 544km/h, she covered the 304.8m in a blink-and-you'll-miss-it 3.659 seconds. Drag racing is about two things: acceleration and speed. Two cars line up beside each other then race head-to-head to cover the dead-straight track and cross the finish line in the quickest time.

Top Fuel dragsters (sometimes called 'rails' because of their long and narrow appearance) are the fastest accelerating cars in the world. From a dead stop, they can reach 160km/h in less than a second, meaning that drivers experience forces similar to those of astronauts when they blast into space in a rocket. A rear-fitted V8 engine injected with **nitromethane** fuel provides the power, two chunky tyres provide the

traction, and an airfoil 'wing' creates the downforce needed to stop the vehicle from literally taking off into the air. Before they race, drivers often perform a 'burnout' by spinning their rear wheels while keeping the car stationary; the friction heats the tyres and gives them more grip. The fire that sometimes bursts from a dragster's exhaust pipes is called 'header flame', or 'bunny ears'. Just as they need to speed up quickly, dragsters need to slow down quickly, too. After crossing the finish line, drivers slam on powerful brakes and release two parachutes. As well as creating **drag** to reduce speed, the parachutes also keep the car stable as it decelerates to a stop. Drag racing is a dangerous motorsport and crashes, when they happen, are spectacular. Because of this, drivers wear fireproof suits, face masks and helmets, and their cars are fitted with safety equipment including fire extinguishers and damage-resistant fuel tanks.

SPECIALIST CARS

As we have seen throughout this book, automobiles are incredibly versatile vehicles. New car types can be designed from scratch, or standard models can be heavily modified to be used for specific or specialised purposes. Bigger engines, bigger wheels, more gears, more lights, special materials, special decorations... the list of modifications to make the automobile fit the job is almost endless.

Police officers use patrol cars to chase suspects, speed to incident or accident sites and cruise the streets looking for suspicious activity or people who need help. Their bright paint schemes and 'police' **decals** are designed to deter criminal activity. Patrol cars are equipped with sirens and flashing lightbars to warn people of their approach, radios to communicate with colleagues, dashboard-mounted cameras, loudspeakers and directional spotlights. Onboard computers allow officers to write incident reports, get information on suspects and check number plates.

The President of the USA is one of the most high profile people in the world, so they need a car that will protect them during any kind of emergency. The presidential state car – or the 'Beast' as it is sometimes called – is a custom built Cadillac that weighs 7.5 tons. Many of its defensive features are kept secret. It's thought to have 13-cm-thick bulletproof windows, 20-cm-thick doors and an **airtight** interior to protect against chemical attacks. The reinforced chassis is bombproof, the tyres are bulletproof and can still run when flat and there are bags of the President's blood on board in case they need a transfusion. The Beast is driven by a specially trained secret service agent.

MILITARY CARS

Automobiles of one type or other have been used by armies almost from the time they were first invented. They can be used to transport soldiers and equipment faster than horses – and they don't need anywhere near as much care and attention. They can be armoured to protect those inside, designed to cope with difficult terrain and have weapons added to turn them into effective fighting machines.

The first armoured cars appeared in the early 1900s and were usually ordinary automobiles with armour and weapons bolted to the outside (which often made them look quite odd); by the Second World War, armored cars were being specially designed. Unlike tanks, they run on wheels instead of caterpillar tracks. Their role is usually to scout ahead, observe enemy activity and provide protection for vulnerable infantry. The American-designed M8 'Greyhound' (pictured) has six wheels, a long range radio set, a 37mm main gun plus two machine guns, a top speed of 90km/h, a range of 560km and has been used by armed forces from 1945 right up to the present day.

After the First World War, governments realised they needed a light military vehicle that could quickly travel long distances over harsh and wartorn terrain. Many chose motorbikes as a solution. The American government decided to design something new – the Jeep. This ¼ ton, four-wheel drive vehicle, powered by a 2.2l Willys 'Go Devil' engine was tough, durable and versatile. Jeeps could go anywhere, transporting people and hauling equipment much faster than the horses they replaced. Over 600,000 were built between 1941 and 1945, and the Jeep led directly to modern off-road vehicles and SUVs (see page 12).

INTO THE FUTURE

There are around 1.42 billion cars in the world, and that number is growing. About 98% burn non-renewable fossil fuels, and emit a staggering 2.23 billion tons of carbon dioxide (plus other greenhouse gasses) into our atmosphere every year. This pollution is heating the Earth, and badly affects our health and the environment. Fortunately, practical alternatives are being developed to help our planet.

Battery-powered electric vehicles (EVs) are becoming ever more popular and will most likely replace fossil-fuel-burning automobiles in the coming decades. Developed and sold by most of the major manufacturers, EVs are quiet, smooth, cheap to run, don't produce harmful emissions and can be recharged at home or at public **charging points**. Battery technology is improving all the time, and most modern EVs can travel around 300km before needing to recharge.

Biofuels such as bioethanol and biodiesel are another alternative. Unlike fossil fuels, biofuels come from **renewable** sources such as vegetable oil, corn and sugarcane, and they don't produce as much pollution. Hydrogen-powered Fuel Cell Electric Vehicles (FCEVs) don't create any emissions, but presently the fuel cell technology is too expensive to be practical.

Some automobile and technology companies are developing self-driving cars (also called 'autonomous vehicles' or 'AVs'). AVs have computers and sensors onboard that do the job of a human driver. The computer knows its local area, including roads, traffic lights and speed limits. The sensors provide information on the car's immediate surroundings, including pedestrians and other vehicles. Although some cities have driverless taxi services, there are difficulties to overcome (such as developing computers capable of safely navigating very busy streets) before AVs can become widely used.

AUTOMOBILE TIMELINE

Since its invention in the 1800s, the automobile has become the most produced vehicle in history. Practical, versatile and giving people complete freedom to travel, the automobile is here to stay. And who knows what the future holds for this amazing machine?

1801

Puffing Devil is the first steam-powered road vehicle, carrying six passengers and travelling at 8km/h.

1885

The Motorwagen is the first automobile powered by an internal combustion engine, designed by Karl Benz.

1885

The first petrol-powered motorcycle is invented in Germany, called the Reitwagen.

1888

The Flocken Elektrowagen is designed, one of the first electric cars.

1927

The Sunbeam 1000hp becomes first automobile to travel at 328km/h.

1937

The Golden Gate Bridge is finished.

1938

The Buick Y-Job is the first concept car.

1940s

The first drive-through restaurant opens in the USA – Red's Giant Hamburg.

1950

The first Formula One race is held at Silverstone, UK.

1958

Seatbelts are included as a standard feature in cars.

1975

Bob Chandler invents the very first Monster Truck, Bigfoot®.

1992

The Interstate Highway System is complete in the USA.

1895
The first truck is invented by Karl Benz.

1901
The Oldsmobile Model R Curved Dash becomes the first mass-produced car.

1907
The first Isle of Man TT race is held.

1911
The first Monte Carlo Rally is held.

1920s
The mass production of cars is in full swing.

1923
The first 24 Hours of Le Mans race is held.

1924
The doble steam car is designed, one of the last advanced steam automobiles.

1926
Route 66 in the USA is completed.

2000s
An average of 64 million cars were made worldwide between 2000 and 2010.

2012
The electric automotive car factory Tesla launches its flagship Model S vehicle.

2020
Electric cars take off. More than one million were on the road worldwide.

1997
The ThrustSSC reaches 1,228km/h, breaking the sound barrier.

RECORD BREAKERS

The long history of the automobile has seen records made and broken many times over, and because technology never stops advancing it's clear there are more still to come. Here are a few of the greatest.

LONGEST CAR JUMP

82m / Subaru Impreza / Travis Pastrana / 2009 / California, USA

MOST EXPENSIVE CAR SOLD

Ferrari 250 GTO / £53 million / 2018

LAND SPEED RECORD

1,228km/h / ThrustSSC / Andy Green / Black Rock Desert, USA

WORLD'S SHORTEST HIGHWAY

Chandler Highway / 1.4km / Melbourne, Australia

BESTSELLING CAR

Toyota Corolla / 50 million units and counting

HEAVIEST CAR

ZIL-41047 Stretched Limousine / 6 tons / Russia

LONGEST CAR

Custom-built limousine / 30.5m / 26 wheels / USA

LONGEST SIDE WHEELIE

371km / BMW 316 / Michele Pilia / 2009 / Italy

FASTEST POLICE CAR

Bugatti Veyron / 407km/h / Dubai Police / United Arab Emirates

GLOSSARY

ACCELERATION

A vehicle's capacity to gain speed. Affected by engine power, weight and aerodynamics.

AERODYNAMIC

Vehicles designed to be less affected by drag. Aerodynamic vehicles often have smooth, narrow or rounded bodies so air flows more easily over them.

AIRTIGHT

An object that is sealed so that air (or water) cannot escape or get in.

BUTTERFLY DOORS

Automobile doors that open upwards like wings. Sometimes found on sports cars, they allow for easier entry and exit.

CHARGING POINTS

An energy source that allows drivers to recharge the battery of their electric or hybrid vehicle.

CHASSIS

The base frame for a vehicle, to which all other components, such as the wheels, engine and body are attached.

CONGESTION

Build-up of traffic on roads, resulting in stationary or slow-moving vehicles, and longer journey times.

CONTOURS

The outline, form or shape of an object.

DECALS

Colourful stickers. Often used on racing cars by companies sponsoring the team.

DRAG

A force that slows a vehicle down. Caused by disruptive airflow over the vehicle's body.

EMISSIONS

Harmful waste gases, such as carbon dioxide and carbon monoxide, created when vehicles burn fossil fuels. Emissions can cause respiratory diseases in people and contribute to climate change.

FENDERS

Rails or covers fixed to the front and back of a vehicle to lessen injury to pedestrians and protect the vehicle's body during collisions. Also called 'bumpers'.

FOSSIL FUEL

Vehicle fuels such as petrol and diesel that are refined from oil drilled from underground. Burning fossil fuels damages the environment and contributes to climate change.

HAIRPIN BENDS

Very tight U-shaped bends in a road.

MECHANICS

People trained to repair, maintain and make improvements to automobiles.

NITROMETHANE

An explosive liquid containing the chemicals nitrogen and oxygen. Used as a fuel in Top Fuel dragsters.

NOSE CONE

The front part of an aerodynamically designed automobile.

PANNIERS

Small luggage cases hung from the sides of motorbikes.

PEDESTRIAN

A person walking rather than taking a form of transport.

RENEWABLE

Energy that comes from a source that doesn't run out, such as wind or solar power.

ROLL CAGES

Protective metal frames inside the body of a car. Used in rally cars, they are designed to protect the driver and passengers if the vehicle rolls over.

STABILITY

A vehicle's ability to resist disruptive external forces such as high winds or winding roads. Stable cars are easier to control.

STRAIGHTS

Sections of a road without any bends or curves.

SUPERCAPACITORS

Devices that can store large amounts of electric energy.

SUSPENSION

The springs and shock absorbers used to attach the wheels to the chassis. Along with air-filled tyres, they create a smoother ride over uneven surfaces.

TAILFINS

Decorative extensions to the rear of a car's body to give a stylish, aerodynamic look. Popular on American vehicles of the 1950–60s.

TRACTION

The grip an automobile's tyre has on the driving surface. Tyres with more traction are less likely to slide, skid or slip.

WATERLOGGED

Something that is covered or saturated with water.

INDEX

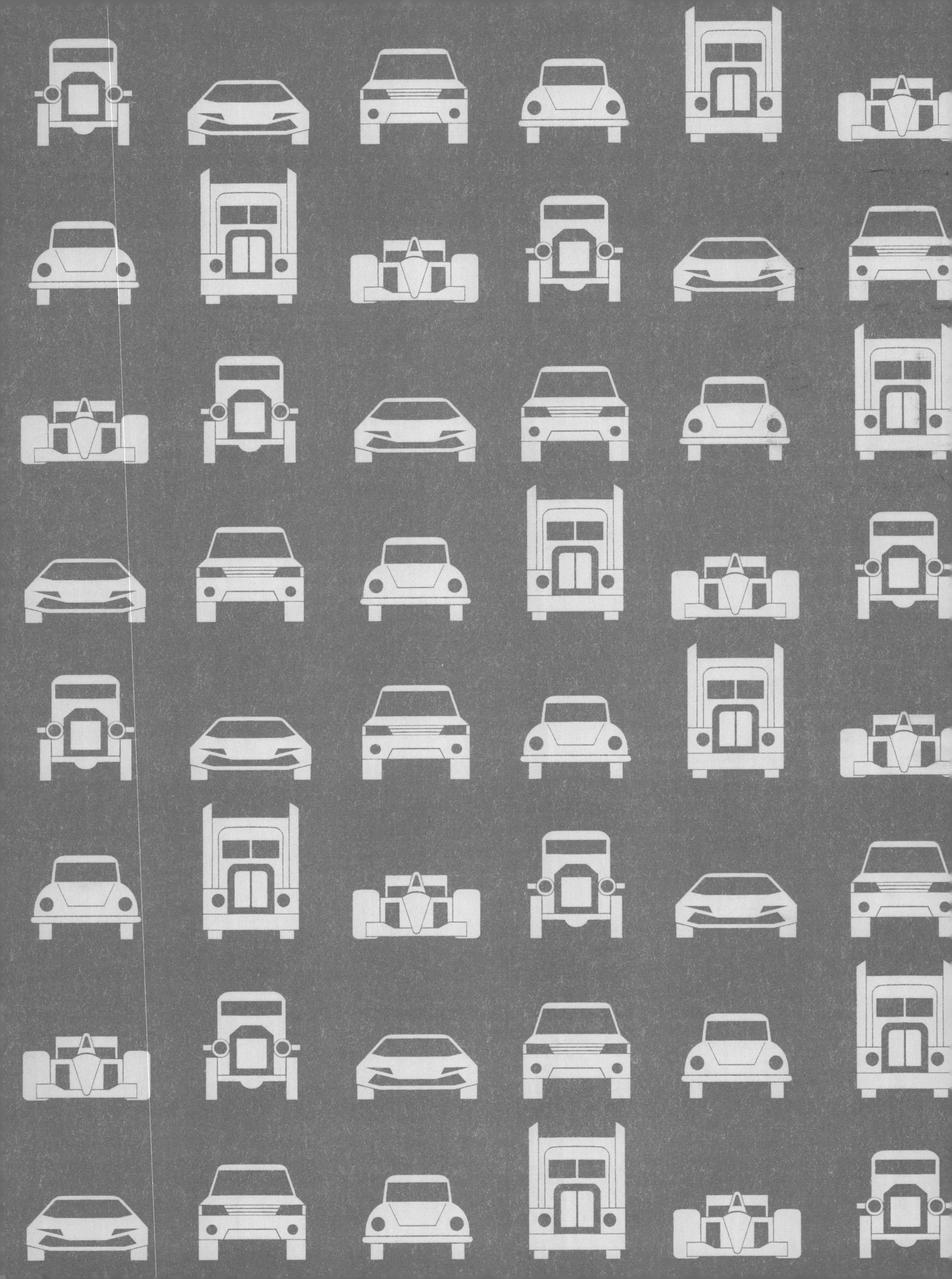